Twin Spin: 17 Shakespeare Sonnets

Radically translated by Ulrike Draesner
Back-translated by Tom Cheesman

With an Exhibition Catalogue for

Shall I compare thee?
Shakespeare in Translation

Taylor Institution Library, Oxford, 2016

Twin Spin: 17 Shakespeare Sonnets
Radically translated by Ulrike Draesner
Back-translated by Tom Cheesman
Edited by Henrike Lähnemann and Emma Huber
Published in 2016 by the Taylor Institution Library, Oxford
With a catalogue for the exhibition
Shall I compare thee? Shakespeare in Translation
Trinity Term 2016, Voltaire Room

The poems by Draesner and Cheesman are reprinted
with minor emendations from *Thymine*,
published by Hafan Books, Swansea, 2013
(Boiled String Poetry Chapbooks # 7) by permission

ISBN 978-0-9954564-0-2

All images are based on the facsimile edition by Sidney Lee,
Shakespeares Sonnets, Oxford 1905 (available on archive.org) which
reproduces the Bodleian copy of the first edition of the sonnets:
Shake-speares Sonnets. Neuer before imprinted, London: 1609,
Oxford, Bodleian Library: Arch. G d.41 (2).

Copyright © Taylor Institution Library 2016
St Giles, Oxford, OX1 3NA
http://www.bodleian.ox.ac.uk/taylor

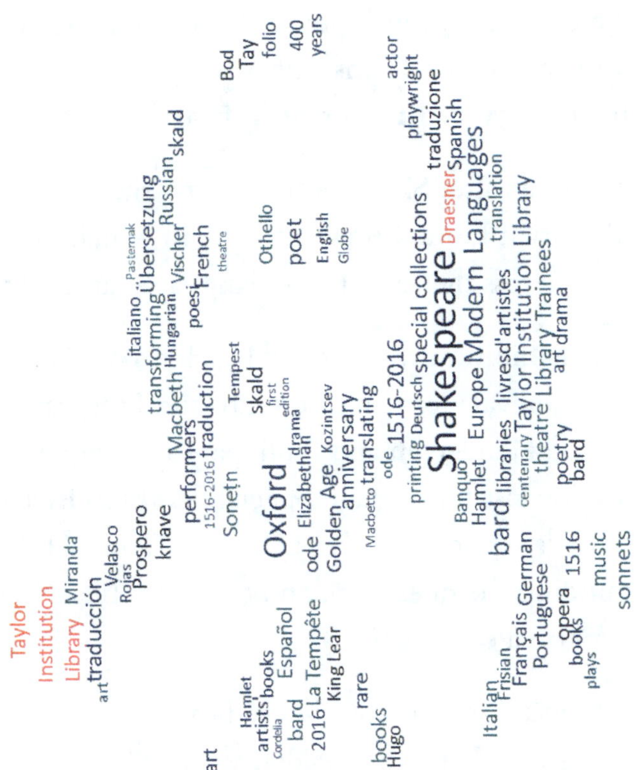

Shall I compare thee?

Shakespeare in Translation

Exhibition Trinity Term 2016
Voltaire Room
Taylor Institution Library, Oxford

Celebrating Shakespeare, Ulrike Draesner and the Art of Translation in the Taylor Institution Library

400 years after Shakespeare's death, the Taylorian Library presents ways in which his texts have stayed alive across the centuries in languages around the world.

The exhibition was curated by Henrike Lähnemann (Professor of Medieval German Literature and Linguistics), together with Emilia Henderson and Philippa Taylor and the help of the Taylor Institution staff. Special thanks to Lydia Pryce-Jones who designed the cover image, to Emma Huber for master-minding the operation, and to Clare Hills-Nova for her curatorial expertise!

A special focus lies on the "radical translation" by Ulrike Draesner, Writer in Residence in Oxford, on the occasion of the symposium discussing her work in April 2016 (Case 1).

The European obsession with translating Shakespeare's sonnets is shown in copies from the Taylorian holdings from the 19th to the 21st century. (Case 2 – Case 4)

The worldwide context of Shakespeare-mania is explored in other forms of creative adaptation, across languages and media. A special case is provided by the Tempest which is presented both in visual and linguistic transformations. (Case 5 – Case 6)

Case 1: Shakespeare x Draesner x Cheesman

The genesis of 'Twin Spin' lies in the cloning debate of the 1990's when Ulrike Draesner wrote the essay 'Will and Dolly', published with 17 'radical translations' in 2000. Tom Cheesman picked up the ball with his back-translations, published together with Ulrike Draesner's versions and Olive 

Ond's *Shakespeare's sonnets spun through 7 languages with GoogleTranslate* as 'Thymine' in 2013. The newest transformation goes back to the oldest form of reproduction: handpress printing.

1 *Twin Spin: 17 Shakespeare Sonnets*
   radically translated by Ulrike Draesner
   and back-translated by Tom Cheesman
   ed. by Henrike Lähnemann and Emma Huber
   Taylor Institution Library, Oxford: 2016
   Taylor Institution Library Depositum

2 *Thymine*, 17 Sonnets x 4 by
   William Shakespeare, Ulrike Draesner, Tom Cheesman, Olive Ond
   Hafan Books, Swansea: 2013
   (Boiled String Poetry Chapbooks # 7)
   Taylor Institution Library Depositum

3 *To change the subject. Die Übersetzung der Worte in Sprache*
   ed. by Peter Waterhouse
   with: Ulrike Draesner: Twin Spin, Sonette von Shakespeare
   and: Barbara Köhler: Niemands Frau, Gesänge zur Odyssee
   Wallstein, Göttingen: 2000
   Taylor Institution Library REP.G.14145

4 *Sonnet 68: Shakespeare x Draesner*
   Typeset by staff and students from Modern Languages
   Handprinted by Ulrike Draesner,
   Bibliographic Press, Bodleian Library: March 2016

Case 2: German Sonnet Translations

After the Bible, Shakespeare's sonnets are the work of world literature most often translated into German. Indeed, it has become a touchstone for any self-respecting poet to provide a new translation of at least the best known – sonnet 18 racks up more than 200 translations. The Taylorian presents a small selection, starting with Dorothea Tieck, and shows the library's multiple copies of the typographically opulent version by Stefan George.

XVIII

Soll ich vergleichen einem sommertage
Dich der du lieblicher und milder bist?
Das maien teure knospen drehn im schlage
Des sturms und allzukurz ist sommers frist.

Des himmels aug scheint manchmal bis zum brennen·
Trägt goldne farbe die sich oft verliert·
Jed schön will sich vom schönen manchmal trennen
Durch zufall oder wechsels lauf entziert.

Doch soll dein ewiger sommer nie ermatten:
Dein schönes sei vor dem verlust gefeit.
Nie prahle Tod· du gingst in seinem schatten..
In ewigen reimen ragst du in die zeit.

Solang als menschen atmen· augen sehn
Wird dies und du der darin lebt bestehn.

1   *Shakespeares Sonette: in der Übersetzung Dorothea Tiecks*
ed. by Christa Jansohn, Tübingen, Francke: 1992
Taylor Institution Library REP.G.6068

2   Otto Gildemeister: *Shakespeare's Sonette*
Brockhaus, Leipzig 1876
Taylor Institution Library 17.G.18

3   Stefan George: *Shakespeare sonnette*
Georg Bondi, Berlin: 1909 et al.
Taylor Institution Library LU.226.A.16(12) /
CB.GEO6 – 4 – J2 *12

4   Friedrich Huch: *Shakespeare, Sonette: ins Deutsche übertragen*
von Paul Renner mit einer Titelzeichnung und Initialen geschmückt
Georg Müller, München 1921
Taylor Institution Library Donation Angi Howell 2013

5   Karl Kraus: *Shakespeare's Sonette*
Kösel: München 1964
Taylor Institution Library MC.401.A.1

6   Wolf Biermann: *Das ist die feinste Liebeskunst: 40 Shakespeare-Sonette*
Kiepenheuer & Witsch: Köln, 2004
Taylor Institution Library SC.9094.A.12

Case 3: Editing & Researching the Sonnets

Researching Shakespeare's sonnets has been done nearly as often as translating them. European academics tended to be less obsessed with the name game of the addressee, and more focussed on the sonnets as reflecting the status of poetry. Comparing different translations has proved a popular past-time, compiling, classifying and contrasting varying takes on the form, content and poetical concepts behind them.

1   Friedrich Theodor Vischer: *Shakespeare-Vorträge*, vol. 1
    J.G. Cotta, Stuttgart: 1899
            Taylor Institution Library HG.295.A.1

2   Georg Gottfried Gervinus: *Shakespeare*
    W. Engelmann, Leipzig: 1862
            Taylor Institution Library 47.F.21

3   Karl Joseph Simrock: *Die Quellen des Shakspeare in Novellen, Märchen
    und Sagen mit sagengeschichtlichen Nachweisungen*
    A. Marcus, Bonn: 1870
            Taylor Institution Library 47.D.13/14

4   Ludwig W. Kahn: *Shakespeares Sonette in Deutschland:
    Versuch einer literarischen Typologie*. Thesis 1934; published:
    Gotthelf Verlag: Bern und Leipzig, 1935
            Taylor Institution Library M. adds. 95 d.22 /
    REP.G.15146

5   Ulrich Erckenbrecht: *Shakespeare Sechsundsechzig
    200 deutsche Übersetzungen von Sonett 66*
    3rd edition, Muriverlag, Kassel: 2009
            Taylor Institution Library TNR 63369

Case 4: European Sonnet Translations

Beyond Germany, Shakespeare's sonnets have also invited poets in
other countries to identify with them – in particular, Yiddish and
Russian versions reveal the sonnets as a secret code to talk about a life
led under dictatorship or in exile. In France, François-Victor Hugo
engages in a dialogue with Shakespeare. In Italy, Giuseppe
Ungaretti's version can also be read in this way, as expressed in the
title of a dissertation on his translation: 'Da poeta a poeta'.

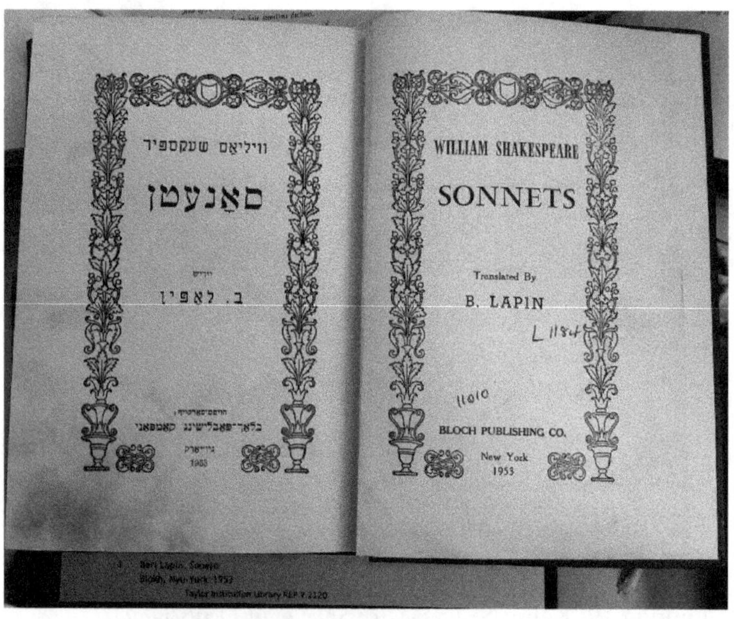

1   Berl Lapin: *Sonetn.* Blokh, Nyu-Yorḳ: 1953
                 Taylor Institution Library REP.Y.2120

2   Giuseppe Ungaretti: *40 sonetti di Shakespeare.*
         Mondadori, Milan: 1966
                 Taylor Institution Library CIR.6148.A.1

3   Antonietta Cataldi: *Da poeta a poeta: il sonetto XXXIII di Shakespeare
         nelle traduzioni di Montale e Ungaretti*
         Congedo, Galatina (Lecce): 1996
                 Taylor Institution Library REP.I.5563

4   Ramón Gutiérrez Izquierdo: *Sonetos de Shakespeare: Shakespeare's sonnets*. Edicións Xerais de Galicia, Vigo: 2011
         Taylor Institution Library Closed Stacks

5   Joan Triadú: *Els sonets de Shakespeare: estudi i selecció d'interpretacions*
         Els cinquanta-cinc, Barcelona: 1958
         Taylor Institution Library REP.S.118

6   Sergei Marshak: *Izbrannye perevody angliĭskie ballady i pesni*.
         Moscow: Gos. izd-vo khudozh. lit-ry 1946
         Taylor Slavonic Library PG3476.M3725.A6.I9

7   S.I. Trukhanov: *Sonety*. Moscow: 2003
         Taylor Slavonic Library TNR 15706

8   Albert Wawrik: *Dwě lubosći ja mam : 77 sonetow* (Sorbian translation with an introduction by Gerald Stone). Budyšin : Domowina 1989
         Taylor Slavonic Library PG3476.M3725.A6.I9

9   Jan Vladsilav: *Sonety* | [Vyd. 2] | Praha : Mladá fronta 1964
         Taylor Slavonic Library TNR24286

Case 5: Shakespeare Translated Across Media

Translation is not confined to the page. Shakespeare has inspired visualisations from early illustrations to video installations. In this section, the Taylorian librarians have put together some suggestions

for further explorations of the Bard's rich heritage across the world –
an invitation to go on further explorations in the stacks, shelves and
displays across the building!

1   **Korol' Lir [videorecording]** Kozint͡sev, Grigoriĭ Mikhaĭlovich ;
       Pasternak, Boris Leonidovich, 1890-1960 ; Shostakovich, Dmitriĭ
       Dmitrievich, 1906-1975   2004 [S.l.] : Russian Cinema Council 2
       DVDs (140 min.)
       Taylor Institution Library PN.R9.K69 KOR DVD-S

2   **Macbetto: tragedia di G. Shakspeare** Leoni, Michele, 1776-1858 ;
       Capurro, Niccolò   1815 Pisa : Presso Niccolò Capurro 162
       Taylor Institution Library VET.ITAL.IV.B.881

3   **O rei Lear** Shakespeare, William, 1564-1616. Vieira,
       Manuel   1943 Coimbra : Editorial Saber 271 p. : ports. ; 19 cm
       Taylor Institution Library REP.P.218

4   'Macbeth' – illustration (Livres d'Artistes), Gromaire, Marcel, 1892-
       1971; Shakespeare, William (translated by François-Victor Hugo).
       Paris, Tériade, 1958.
       Taylor Institution Library, Strachan Collection

5   **Otello: Maour Venezia** Klerg, Marsel, 1912-1984   2007 Kemper
       [i.e. Quimper] : Embann. al Lanv 197 p. : 18 cm
       Taylor Institution Library Closed Stack

6   **Macbeth: tragédie en cinq actes** Ducis, J.-F. (Jean-François),
       1733-1816.   1816 Paris : A. Nepveu 86 p. 20 cm
       Taylor Institution Library VET.FR.III.B.572

7   **Hamlet: tragédie en cinq actes, imitée de l'anglais** Ducis, J.-F.
       (Jean-François), 1733-1816.   1813 Nouv. éd., augm. des variantes.
       Paris : A. Nepveu 88 p. ; 21 cm
       Taylor Institution Library FINCH.M.126(2)

8   **Romeo y Julieta; Otelo** Neruda, Pablo, 1904-1973 ; Macpherson,
       Guillermo, 1824-1898 ; Henríquez Ureña, Pedro, 1884-1946   1966
       Buenos Aires : Losada 217 p. ; 18 cm
       Taylor Institution Library RPM-NER.242/1

9   Dramas de Guillermo Shakespeare : El mercader de Venecia ;
     Macbeth ; Romeo y Julieta ; Otelo : dibujos y grabados al boj de
     los principales artistas alemanes Menéndez y Pelayo, Marcelino,
     1856–1912   1881 Barcelona : Biblioteca "Arte y Letras"
                 Taylor Institution Library REP.S.2665

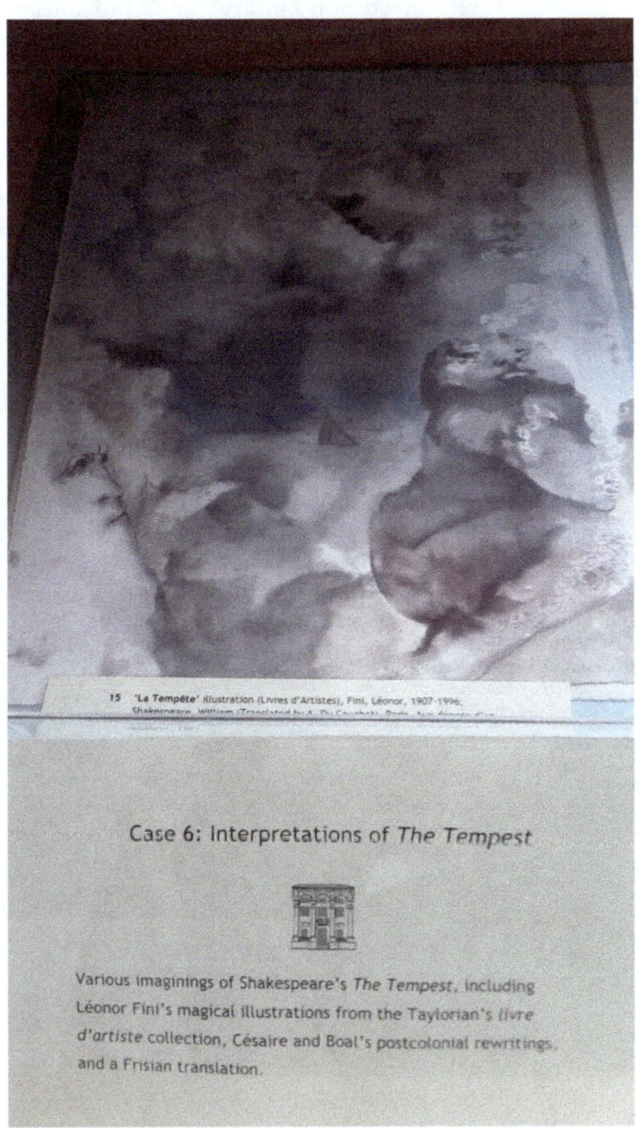

Case 6: Interpretations of the Tempest

1   **'La Tempête'** illustration (Livres d'Artistes), Fini, Léonor, 1907–1996; Shakespeare, William (Translated by A. Du Couchet). Paris, Aux dépens d'un amateur, 1965.

        Taylor Institution Library, Strachan Collection

2   **A tempestade; As mulheres de atenas** Boal, Augusto. 1977 Lisboa : Plátano Editora 204 p. ; 18 cm

        Taylor Institution Library DAF.2.BOA

3   **Une tempête: theatre : d'après "La tempête" de Shakespeare. Adaptation pour un théâtre nègre.** Césaire, Aimé. [1969] Paris : Éditions du Seuil 93 p. ; 18 cm

        Taylor Institution Library DFE.2.CES.A.204/1

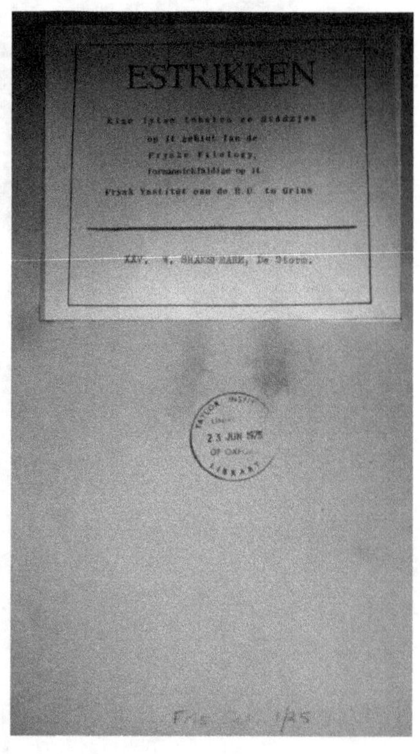

4   **De storm: in toneelstik:** Posthumus, Rinse, 1790–1859 1958 Grins: Frysk Ynstitút oan de R. U. to Grins

        Taylor Institution Library FRIS.SER.1/23

SHAKE-SPEARES

SONNETS.

Neuer before Imprinted.

Shakespeare x Draesner

Shakespeare x Draesner x Cheesman

AT LONDON
By *G. Eld* for *T. T.* and are
to be folde by *William Afpley.*
1609.

FRom faireſt creatures we deſire increaſe,
That thereby beauties *Roſe* might neuer die,
But as the riper ſhould by time deceaſe,
His tender heire might beare his memory:
But thou contracted to thine owne bright eyes,
Feed'ſt thy lights flame with ſelfe ſubſtantiall fewell,
Making a famine where aboundance lies,
Thy ſelfe thy foe,to thy ſweet ſelfe too cruell:
Thou that art now the worlds freſh ornament,
And only herauld to the gaudy ſpring,
Within thine owne bud burieſt thy content,
And tender chorle makſt waſt in niggarding:
    Pitty the world,or elſe this glutton be,
    To eate the worlds due,by the graue and thee.

1 Shakespeare

From fairest creatures we desire increase,
That thereby beauty's rose might never die,
But as the riper should by time decrease,
His tender heir might bear his memory:
But thou, contracted to thine own bright eyes,
Feed'st thy light's flame with self-substantial fuel,
Making a famine where abundance lies,
Thyself thy foe, to thy sweet self too cruel.
Thou that art now the world's fresh ornament,
And only herald to the gaudy spring,
Within thine own bud buriest thy content,
And, tender churl, mak'st waste in niggarding.
    Pity the world, or else this glutton be,
    To eat the world's due, by the grave and thee.

1 Shakespeare x Draesner

von hellsten kreaturen begehren wir anstieg
dass das mandelbrot der gekrümmten schönheit nie sterbe
doch wie die fertigen mit der zeit verschwinden, so mag ein kopierer
belockend die erinnerung an sie tragen: in sich.
du aber, getackert an die schlauheit deiner augen
fütterst die flamme des anscheins mit dem selbst
referentiellen öl der sprache des einzelnen
wo überfluss zu zellen gerinnt, bist dir mit dir
genug, das ornament dieser welt: naturident
blühn im kasten die karten deines kontinents
auf, durch deinen glasstabkörper, steigt sie längst
im spendesaal, die zarte locke dna.
    bedaure die gezeugten, sonst ist es antropophagie
    das ihre zu essen, wie ihr grab, behandelst du sie.

1 Shakespeare x Draesner x Cheesman

of brightest creatures we desire returns,
that the mandelbrot of crooked beauty never die,
but the readied timely fading, a copier or heir
can carry their tender memory curling within them:
you however, fastened to the cuteness of your own eyes,
feed the flambeau semblance with the self
referential oil of a language one solely owns,
where excess reduces to cells, do you for you
suffice, this world's adornment: synth-nature
slide-arrayed, the charting of your continent is up
wards through your glass-rod-body churns already,
donor-spent, the curly tendril dna.
pity the procreated, or else a cannibal be, eat the m
eat of them, like their grave, should you treat the m.

5.

THose howers that with gentle worke did frame,
  The louely gaze where euery eye doth dwell
Will play the tirants to the very same,

                                        And

SONNETS.

And that vnfaire which fairely doth excell:
For neuer resting time leads Summer on,
To hidious winter and confounds him there,
Sap checkt with frost and lustie leau's quite gon,
Beauty ore-snow'd and barenes euery where,
Then were not summers distillation left
A liquid prisoner pent in walls of glasse,
Beauties effect with beauty were bereft,
Nor it nor noe remembrance what it was.
    But flowers distil'd though they with winter meete,
    Leese but their show,their substance still liues sweet.

5 Shakespeare

Those hours that with gentle work did frame
The lovely gaze where every eye doth dwell,
Will play the tyrants to the very same,
And that unfair which fairly doth excel;
For never-resting Time leads summer on
To hideous winter, and confounds him there;
Sap check'd with frost, and lusty leaves quite gone,
Beauty o'versnow'd, and bareness everywhere:
Then, were not summer's distillation left,
A liquid prisoner pent in walls of glass,
Beauty's effect with beauty were bereft,
Nor it, nor no remembrance what it was.
    But flowers distill'd, though they with winter meet,
    Leese but their show; their substance still lives sweet.

5 Shakespeare x Draesner

die stunden, die mit weichem mull den rahmen spannten
deines blicks, in dem so gern ein fremdes auge schwimmt
werden die transplanteure geben, als sich, an dich
und ausgeleuchtet wird, was das leuchtendste übertraf:
die in atomen tickende zeit überführt den sommer
in strahlenderen winter, und zergründet ihn dort:
saft, im kühlschrank erstarrt, fleischige membranen, welk
schönheit überkrustet von frost, nacktheit, an jedem ort:
stünde dann nicht das destillat des sommers im fach
flüssiger gefangener zwischen wänden und gas
wäre die fruchtblase der schönheit durch schönheit zerstoben
weder sie, noch erinnerung bliebe, daran, was war.
    aber blumenartiges, extrahiert, in den winter geschoben
schwappt als zellcode, milchiger saft, die zukunft ans glas.

5 Shakespeare x Draesner x Cheesman

those hours that spun soft gauze to frame your gaze,
in which an alter eye so gladly swims,
will give transplanters, as themselves, to you,
arc-lighting what out-lit the fullest flood;
for ticking-in-atoms time renders summer up
to glow-in-the-darker winter, and unbases it there:
juice, rimed in the fridge, tissuey membranes, shrunk,
beauty hoar-crusted, nakedness at all points:
stood not then the essence of summer in the chiller,
liquid prisoner twixt walls and gas,
were beauty's amniotic sac by beauty vaporized,
neither it nor memory 'd be left of what was.
but flower-like-ness, extracted, jammed into winter's dry ice,
sloshes as cell-code, milky juice, the future gainst the glass.

6
THen let not winters wragged hand deface,
In thee thy summer ere thou be diftil'd:
Make fweet fome viall;treafure thou fome place,
With beautits treafure ere it be felfe kil'd:
That vfe is not forbidden vfery,
Which happies thofe that pay the willing lone;
That's for thy felfe to breed an other thee,
Or ten times happier be it ten for one,
Ten times thy felfe were happier then thou art,
If ten of thine ten times refigur'd thee,
Then what could death doe if thou fhould'ft depart,
Leauing thee liuing in pofterity?
Be not felfe-wild for thou art much too faire,
To be deaths conqueft and make wormes thine heire,

6 Shakespeare

Then let not winter's ragged hand deface
In thee thy summer, ere thou be distill'd:
Make sweet some phial; treasure thou some place
With beauty's treasure, ere it be self-kill'd.
That use is not forbidden usury,
Which happies those that pay the willing loan;
That's for thyself to breed another thee,
Or ten times happier, be it ten for one;
Ten times thyself were happier than thou art,
If ten of thine ten times refigur'd thee:
Then what could Death do if thou shouldst depart,
Leaving thee living in posterity?
 Be not self-will'd, for thou art much too fair
 To be Death's conquest and make worms thine heir.

6 Shakespeare x Draesner

lass die zerfurchte hand des weißkittligen dein gesicht
nicht auslöschen in dir deine brut, sonst wirst du in stille gewickelt –
füll vorher irgendeine phiole mit schwammigem, alphabetisiere eine stelle
mit den zählbaren buchstaben der helix, bevor auch sie getötet wird.
dieser gebrauch deiner bedeutung ist kein verbotenes wuchern
es beglückt diejenigen, die willig den zins zahlen
es ist deine aufgabe, dir ein anderes du zu züchten
oder zehnmal so glücklich wären, brütete man zehn aus dir
diese zehn mal du glücklicher als du bist
wenn zehn dus – fleischlich, identisch, – dir folgten:
was könnte dann der tod noch bewirken, wenn er dich holt
und du doch im terrafilm weiterspielst, lebendiges lachen?
　　　sei nicht so einzel-willig, denn du bist viel zu belichtet
　　　um nur wurmresistente silikonschalen zu deinen erben zu machen.

6 Shakespeare x Draesner x Cheesman

　　　let white-coat's gnarly hand not scratch your face
　　　in you your brood, else you'll be swaddled in stillness:
plan ahead, fill some phial with mucus, drill some spot in spelling
　　the numerable letters of the helix, lest even that be killed.
　　　such usage of your gist is no verboten usury,
　　　their happying repays the willing loaners;
　　　it's up to you to breed yourself another you,
　　or make ten times as happy ten from you bred;
　　　those ten times yous happier than you are,
　　if ten yous – fleshily identic – followed you:
what then could death, coming after you, carry off,
when you're playing on live, laughing terra-reality-star?
don't be so mono-minded, zygote, far too bright you shine
for your legatees to be but silicon paps the worms decline.

11

AS fast as thou shalt wane so fast thou grow'st,
In one of thine, from that which thou departest,
And that fresh bloud which yongly thou bestow'st,
Thou maist call thine, when thou from youth conuertest,
Herein liues wisdome, beauty, and increase,
Without this follie, age, and could decay,
If all were minded so, the times should ceafe,
And threescoore yeare would make the world away:
Let thofe whom nature hath not made for store,
Harsh, featurelesse, and rude, barrenly perrish,
Looke whom she best indow'd, she gaue the more;
Which bountious guift thou shouldst in bounty cherrish,
    She caru'd thee for her seale, and ment therby,
    Thou shouldst print more, not let that coppy die.

11 Shakespeare

As fast as thou shalt wane, so fast thou grow'st
In one of thine, from that which thou departest.
And that fresh blood which youngly thou bestow'st,
Thou mayst call thine, when thou from youth convertest.
Herein lives wisdom, beauty, and increase:
Without this, folly, age, and cold decay.
If all were minded so the times should cease,
And threescore years would make the world away.
Let those whom Nature hath not made for store,
Harsh, featureless, and rude, barrenly perish:
Look whom she best endow'd, she gave the more;
Which bounteous gift thou shouldst in bounty cherish;
    She carv'd thee for her seal, and meant thereby
    Thou shouldst print more, nor let that copy die.

11 Shakespeare x Draesner

du schwindest schnell, schnell schwillst du wieder an
aus deinen scheidungen gemixt, ein andrer – du.
wenn deine zellen auf *age* konvertieren, nennst frisches
blut dein, in das du jung dich schmuggelst ein.
noch produzieren deine *nuclei* coolness, fitness, börsenwert
nimm eine sequenz nur weg: bse, alzheimer, krebs bleiben dir.
wären alle so programmiert, keiner flöge mehr durch raum und zeit
schon ein schock jahre machte terra den garaus.
lass die, die die weißkittel nicht zu vererbern erkoren
natefakte, kunstlos und grell, sterben steril:
bei goldenem gamet aber gibt's platin gratis obenauf
deinen bounty-spender kirschrot aufzurichten, gut aufgelegt
    gezüchtet als siegel und sieg, ist zu spuren dir auferlegt
    in tausend anderen; klon und klonesklon, aufgelebt!

11 Shakespeare x Draesner x Cheesman

    you quickly shrink, as quickly swell again
from you-exuded splittings, spliced to mix another – you.
    when your cells convert to age, you claim as yours
fresh blood you trojan horse your self youngingly through.
your nuclei keep producing cool-, fit-, high-dividendedness;
delete a single sequence: bse, alzheimer's, cancer, yours yet.
were all so programmed, none 'd fly on through space-time;
    down a span of years, terra would be trashed.
let those the white-coats won't have as hereditators,
    natefacts, artless and shrill, be sterile and die:
but buy gametal gold, get platinum top-up free;
your cherry-red bounty-bar-donor raised high, be blithe,
    selected as victory-seal, your lot's to thrive
and spoor in a thousand more; clone of a clone, go live!

> **I 5**
>
> VVHen I confider euery thing that growes
>   Holds in perfection but a little moment.
> That this huge ftage prefenteth nought but fhowes
> Whereon the Stars in fecret influence comment.
> When I perceiue that men as plants increafe,
> Cheared and checkt euen by the felfe-fame skie:
> Vaunt in their youthfull fap,at height decreafe,
> And were their braue ftate out of memory.
> Then the conceit of this inconftant ftay,
> Sets you moft rich in youth before my fight,
> Where waftfull time debateth with decay
> To change your day of youth to fullied night,
>   And all in war with Time for loue of you
>   As he takes from you,I ingraft you new.

15 Shakespeare

When I consider every thing that grows
Holds in perfection but a little moment,
That this huge stage presenteth nought but shows
Whereon the stars in secret influence comment;
When I perceive that men as plants increase,
Cheered and check'd even by the self-same sky;
Vaunt in their youthful sap, at height decrease,
And wear their brave state out of memory;
Then the conceit of this inconstant stay
Sets you most rich in youth before my sight,
Where wasteful time debateth with decay,
To change your day of youth to sullied night;
        And, all in war with Time, for love of you,
        As he takes from you, I engraft you new.

15 Shakespeare x Draesner

wenn ich mir ansehe, jedes ding, das wächst
hält sich vollkommen nur für einen augenblick
dass dieser gestaltenball nichts präsentiert als einige pawlow-reflexe
die der verborgne einfluss der filme, augen, tiefkühlcodes kommentiert
wenn ich wahrnehme, dass menschen sich wie pflanzen vermehren
angefeuert und verbrannt von ein und demselben löchrigen himmel
gerühmt als vollsaftig, jung, schrumpfen sie ins kleine zurück
und tragen ihren indie-zustand-b aus der erinnerung heraus
dann stellt das internetbild dieses tramper-hotels
im fett des anfangs dich mir vor augen, während
verschwenderische atome mit ihren elektronen debattieren
um die lichtquanten deiner jugend ins dunkle zu verschießen
    und, ganz und gar überworfen mit zeit, aus liebe zu dir
    während sie an dir frisst, dreh ich dich neu, die retorte, von mir.

15 Shakespeare x Draesner x Cheesman

when i see for myself, every thing that grows
keeps perfect only for a mo,
that this whole show's only pavlovian cond reflexes,
plus hidden commentary, pulls of movies, eyes and deepfreeze codes;
when i realize that human beings multiply like flora,
fired up and toasted by the self-same holey sky;
boasted juicy-full, young, they shrink down small,
and wear their b-stage-rave-beat-rate out of memory;
then a web-pic of this backpack hostel fetches
first fine unsaturated you before my eyes,
while wastrel atoms kick around with their electrons,
to cannon the light quanta of your youth into the dark,
and, totally cloaked in war with time, for love of you,
as it feeds off you, i spin you, test tube mine, anew.

18.

Hall I compare thee to a Summers day?
Thou art more louely and more temperate:
Rough windes do shake the darling buds of Maie,
And Sommers lease hath all too short a date:
Sometime too hot the eye of heauen shines,
And often is his gold complexion dimm'd,
And euery faire from faire some-time declines,
By chance, or natures changing course vntrim'd:
But thy eternall Sommer shall not fade,
Nor loose possession of that faire thou ow'st,
Nor shall death brag thou wandr'st in his shade,
When in eternall lines to time thou grow'st,
      So long as men can breath or eyes can see,
      So long liues this, and this giues life to thee,

18 Shakespeare

Shall I compare thee to a summer's day?
Thou art more lovely and more temperate:
Rough winds do shake the darling buds of May,
And summer's lease hath all too short a date:
Sometime too hot the eye of heaven shines,
And often is his gold complexion dimm'd;
And every fair from fair sometime declines,
By chance, or nature's changing course, untrimm'd;
But thy eternal summer shall not fade,
Nor lose possession of that fair thou owest;
Nor shall Death brag thou wander'st in his shade,
When in eternal lines to time thou growest;
      So long as men can breathe, or eyes can see,
      So long lives this, and this gives life to thee.

18 Shakespeare x Draesner

eines sommertags komparse, du?
gesünder bist du, besser temperiert:
stickstoffwinde nagen die teuren maiknospen an
geleaste sommerzeit fault dattelbraun, zu schnell:
zu viel uv strahlt durchs ozonloch ab und brennt
oft ist der sonne teint von smog verhängt
alles helle beugt periodisch helles in den fall
chaotisch der zufall, genetisch unser roulette;
doch in deinem zeitimmunen sommer tanzt keine zelle den fado
keine verliert, dem du dich verdankst, ihr dna-eldorado
noch wird der tod prahlen, in seinem schatten wandre deine pracht
wenn als buchstabenhelix du der zeit entwächst
    solange einer atmen kann, solange augen sehn
    solange lohnt auch dies und klont dir leben ein.

18 Shakespeare x Draesner x Cheesman

    a summer day and you and recombine?
    you're better for you, quality controlled:
    rough nitrous gusts aggress the precious may-buds,
    and summer's time-share option's all too short-date:
    too much uv glows through the ozone hole and burns,
    and sol's complexion's tanned by frequent smog;
    periodically in the case of brightness bright declines,
    chance-entrammelled chaos is our gene-roulette;
    time-immunized, your summer cells, though, dance no fado,
    none loses its, what you owe you to, el-dna-dorado;
nor 'll loud-mouth death proclaim your glory straggles in his gloom,
    when as double-stranded letter-vines you out-climb time;
    so long as breath is drawn, so long as eyes have sight,
    so long this loan repays its own and clones you life.

19

DEuouring time blunt thou the Lyons pawes,
  And make the earth deuoure her owne sweet brood,
Plucke the keene teeth from the fierce Tygers yawes,
And burne the long liu'd Phœnix in her blood,
Make glad and forry feafons as thou fleet'ft,
And do what ere thou wilt fwift-footed time
To the wide world and all her fading fweets:
But I forbid thee one moft hainous crime,

S O N N E T S.

O carue not with thy howers my loues faire brow,
Nor draw noe lines there with thine antique pen,
Him in thy courfe vntainted doe allow,
For beauties patterne to fucceding men.
    Yet doe thy worft ould Time difpight thy wrong,
    My loue fhall in my verfe euer liue young.

19 Shakespeare

Devouring Time, blunt thou the lion's paws,
And make the earth devour her own sweet brood;
Pluck the keen teeth from the fierce tiger's jaws,
And burn the long-liv'd phœnix in her blood;
Make glad and sorry seasons, as thou fleets,
And do whate'er thou wilt, swift-footed Time,
To the wide world, and all her fading sweets;
But I forbid thee one most heinous crime:
O carve not with thy hours my love's fair brow,
Nor draw no lines there with thine antique pen;
Him in thy course untainted do allow,
For beauty's pattern to succeeding men.
    Yet, do thy worst, old Time: despite thy wrong,
    My love shall in my verse ever live young.

19 Shakespeare x Draesner

schlingerin zeit, stumpf des pferdes kick beim start
heiß asphalt, seine rasenden trabanten verschlingen
den gierigen zahn dem grellen stern aus dem spoiler hau
den zähsten piloten in niki-lauda-blut verbrenn
schlinger froh und trüb die saisonalen strecken
tu, was du willst, rakete zeit, im großen rund
benzingeschwängert ist dein süß; nur einen crash
verbiet ich dir, die lasermesser deiner sekunden
berühren des liebsten chromosomen mir nicht
weg mit deinem altes-eisen-stift
gengesund lass ihn auf deinem nürburgring die runden ziehn
als schönheit formel 1, die nachfahrn in die boxen bringt.
    korrupte zeit, bau 'nen bandencrash, deinen abgeriebenen gummis
        zum trotz
    lebt, was ich liebe, in meinen kulturröhrchen fort und strotzt.

19 Shakespeare x Draesner x Cheesman

wolfing time, stunt the horse's start-kick,
bid hot tarmac wolf down its wheeling satellites,
knock out the pimped-up beamer's greedy grille-tooth,
fry the toughest driver in niki lauda blood;
sylph the mood-swung seasons' circuits, do
what you want, o rocket time, about the great ellipse,
petrol-swollen-bellied sweety; just one crash
i veto, keep your seconds' laser-blades
off my best beloved's chromosomes,
jettison your scrap-iron pen;
gene-clean, let him machine the turns around your monaco,
as beauty formula 1, posterity stalled in the pits.
crash-fixing time, even your balding rubber's worst fit
'll leave my dear living on in my culture media, loving it.

24 Shakespeare

Mine eye hath play'd the painter, and hath stell'd
Thy beauty's form in table of my heart;
My body is the frame wherein 'tis held,
And perspective it is best painter's art.
For through the painter must you see his skill,
To find where your true image pictur'd lies,
Which in my bosom's shop is hanging still,
That hath his windows glazed with thine eyes.
Now see what good turns eyes for eyes have done:
Mine eyes have drawn thy shape, and thine for me
Are windows to my breast, where-through the sun
Delights to peep, to gaze therein on thee;
    Yet eyes this cunning want to grace their art,
     They draw but what they see, know not the heart.

24 Shakespeare x Draesner

mein auge hat sich zum agenten des silbers gemacht, die konturen
deiner helligkeit auf die bromoxide meines innersten receivers geprägt
mein körper ist der rahmen, der dieses negativ hält
entfernung und schnitt heißen die kunst dessen, der filmt.
denn durch den, der die kamera führt, bemerke das kleben des auges
in der beobachterabhängigen welt, unter der dein wirkliches bild
                begraben liegt
und lügt, es, der hund, der im schnellimbiss meiner brust den
                schwanz reckt
die teleschirme seiner augen überzogen mit deinem aufnahmegesicht.
nun schau, wieviele gute drehs augen für augen gemacht haben:
meine augen haben deine dna-linie entrollt, und deine sind
die cyberfenster meiner brust, durch die die halogene der
op-sonnen ihre peep-show halten, und dadurch in dich schaun
      doch augen bewegen ihr wollen zu künstlichen kronen, töricht
      halten sie fest, was sie sehen, kennen das unbelichtete nicht.

24 Shakespeare x Draesner x Cheesman

my eye became silver's agent, fixing your brightness
contours onto my innermost receptor's bromoxide;
this negative, my body frames and montages it,
pulling and cutting being the quick of the film-maker's art.
for through the cameraman's, the eye, d' you see, 's stuck fast
the world of observer-dependency, beneath which your image, the true
one, lies, cur, rod-tailed in the snack-bar of my breast yet,
its eyes' hdtv screens glazed with photogenic you.
just look how many tricks eyes have turned for eyes:
mine have untangled the line of your dna, and your eyes are
the windows (© microsoft) of my breast, through which the ot's
halogen suns perform their peep-show, peeking in at you;
yet eyes their wanting draw towards coronas artificed,
they capture but the seen, what's unlit gets missed.

29

VVHen in disgrace with Fortune and mens eyes,
I all alone beweepe my out-cast state,

And

SONNETS.

And trouble deafe heauen with my bootlesse cries,
And looke vpon my selfe and curse my fate.
Wishing me like to one more rich in hope,
Featur'd like him,like him with friends possest,
Desiring this mans art,and that mans skope,
With what I most inioy contented least,
Yet in these thoughts my selfe almost despising,
Haplye I thinke on thee, and then my state,
(Like to the Larke at breake of daye arising)
From sullen earth sings himns at Heauens gate,
        For thy sweet loue remembred such welth brings,
        That then I skorne to change my state with Kings.

29 Shakespeare

When in disgrace with fortune and men's eyes,
I all alone beweep my outcast state,
And trouble deaf Heaven with my bootless cries,
And look upon myself, and curse my fate,
Wishing me like to one more rich in hope,
Featur'd like him, like him with friends possess'd,
Desiring this man's art, and that man's scope,
With what I most enjoy contented least;
Yet in these thoughts myself almost despising,
Haply I think on thee, – and then my state
(Like to the lark at break of day arising
From sullen earth) sings hymns at heaven's gate;
        For thy sweet love remember'd such wealth brings,
        That then I scorn to change my state with kings'.

29 Shakespeare x Draesner

wenn, ausgespuckt vom glück, kriechend vor menschlichen
augen, allein, ich, meine verwerfungen bewein'
und den krebsstrahlenden deckel der welt mit meinen unbootbaren
              schreien in betrieb setze
und mich selbst ansehe, und mich verfluche, wenn ich
mich mir wünsche wie ihn, um eine hoffnung reicher
mit zügen wie er, wie er von freunden besetzt
des einen können begehre, des anderen spielprogramm
mit dem, was ich am meisten genieße, am unzufriedensten, ich
denke ich bei diesen selbstverachtungsgedanken dann
verschlagen-zufällig an dich – sofort singt
mein zustand (wie die condor am anbruch des tages
vom asphalt hebt) hymnen vor diesem cybertelefon
       erinnerung an deine zukünftige liebe bringt mir die jetons
       eines selbst, das ich mit dir gern tauschte, mein königsich,
              mein glasstabklon.

29 Shakespeare x Draesner x Cheesman

              when, stuck in luck's spittoon, in human eyes
       a worm-cast, all alone, me, I'm bewailing my reprehensibility,
              and booting up the sarcoma-glowing lid above
              with my http-404-fetching cries,
       and i'm looking at myself, and i'm cursing me, when i'm
              wishing me a me like him, one hope the richer,
              with looks like him, like him beset with friends,
       craving this guy's skills, and that guy's game software,
              when i'm what i get most out of least enjoying, me;
       if though i then, amid these self-loathing thought spins,
happen wilily to set my mind on you – at once my mental health
       sings (like the aérospatiale alouette at daybreak lifting
              off the tarmac) phone-phreak hymns à la bill gates;
remembering your future love, i rake the chips in that'll let me own
a self i'd gladly swap with you, king-ego mine, my glass-rod-clone.

> 38
>
> How can my Muſe want ſubiect to inuent
> While thou doſt breath that poor'ſt into my verſe,
> Thine owne ſweet argument,to excellent,
> For euery vulgar paper to rehearſe:
> Oh giue thy ſelfe the thankes if ought in me,
> Worthy peruſal ſtand againſt thy ſight,
> For who's ſo dumbe that cannot write to thee,
> When thou thy ſelfe doſt giue inuention light?
> Be thou the tenth Muſe,ten times more in worth
> Then thoſe old nine which rimers inuocate,
> And he that calls on thee,let him bring forth
>
>   Eternall

> SONNETS.
>
> Eternal numbers to out-liue long date.
>   If my ſlight Muſe doe pleaſe theſe curious daies,
>   The paine be mine,but thine ſhal be the praiſe.

38 Shakespeare

How can my muse want subject to invent,
While thou dost breathe, that pour'st into my verse
Thine own sweet argument, too excellent
For every vulgar paper to rehearse?
O, give thyself the thanks, if aught in me
Worthy perusal stand against thy sight;
For who's so dumb that cannot write to thee,
When thou thyself dost give invention light?
Be thou the tenth muse, ten times more in worth
Than those old nine which rhymers invocate;
And he that calls on thee, let him bring forth
Eternal numbers to outlive long date.
    If my slight muse do please these curious days,
    The pain be mine, but thine shall be the praise.

38 Shakespeare x Draesner

ihrer inventio subjekt fehlt meiner muse wahrlich nicht
solang in meine rhythmuskanäle du deine süßen
variablen ergießt, per *excel* sprengst, kein gängiges
personalpapier wüsste noch, wohin mit dir.
schick dir selbst die dankesmail, falls etwas von mir
durch virustests geschlüpft, dir ins gesicht gerät
wer schon wär so blöd, dich nicht schreiben zu können
wenn du selbst ihn mit inventionen bestrahlst?
sei du die zehnte muse, zehnmal mehr wert
als die alten neun, die reimende schäfer belämmerten
den, der dich entpuppt, den lass sie ausgebärn
die datumslosen genomstrophen der endlosigkeit.
    wenn meine l(e)ichte muse dich pläsiert, in diesen tagen
        neuer gier
    die arbeit im labor lass mir, dein sei der preis, mein dolly-tier.

38 Shakespeare x Draesner x Cheesman

my muse wants nought by way of subject of inventio,
so long as you're still pouring your sweet variables
up my rhythm channels, crashing excel-datasets,
escaping any personnel clerk's irksome paperwork.
email your thanks to you yourself, if anything of mine
hath wriggled through the virus check to hatch your face;
who so lacks gumption he could fail to write you,
when you're gamma-zapping him with your inventions?
be you the tenth muse, ten times value-added-er
than the old-time nine the shepherd rhymers bleated on about;
whoso in vitrios you, make him carry to term
eternity's expiry-dateless genome-jingles.
if my light muse amuses you, these days of neo-greed,
mine be the labwork, yours the prize, my dolly woolly-eared.

53

VVHat is your substance, whereof are you made,
That millions of strange shaddowes on you tend?
Since

SONNETS.

Since euery one, hath euery one, one shade,
And you but one, can euery shaddow lend:
Describe *Adonis* and the counterfet,
Is poorely immitated after you,
On *Hellens* cheeke all art of beautie set,
And you in *Grecian* tires are painted new:
Speake of the spring, and foyzon of the yeare,
The one doth shaddow of your beautie show,
The other as your bountie doth appeare,
And you in euery blessed shape we know.
    In all externall grace you haue some part,
    But you like none, none you for constant heart.

53 Shakespeare

What is your substance, whereof are you made,
That millions of strange shadows on you tend?
Since every one hath, every one, one's shade,
And you, but one, can every shadow lend.
Describe Adonis, and the counterfeit
Is poorly imitated after you:
On Helen's cheek all art of beauty set,
And you in Grecian tires are painted new:
Speak of the spring, and foison of the year;
The one doth shadow of your beauty show,
The other as your bounty doth appear,
And you in every blessed shape we know.
    In all external grace you have some part,
    But you like none, none you, for constant heart.

53 Shakespeare x Draesner

was ist deine substanz, woraus bist du gemacht
dass millionen seltsamer schatten sich auf dir nähren?
da jeder einzelne ihn hat, jeder einzeln, einzelnen schatten
und du, ein einzelner nur, kannst jeden schatten verleihen?
beschreib adonis, und das gequetschte silberbromid seiner lenden
verkommt zu armseliger imitation im vergleich mit dir:
leg helenas gesicht die ganze asa-skala der hellen auf
und du bist in deinem griechischen gummi-overall neu
            in den kasten gebannt
sprich vom anfang und der beute des jahres
der eine trägt die merkmale deiner zellbewegungen
die andere erscheint als die ausscheidung deiner massen
und du, in jeder trächtigen form, die wir dir verpassen
        hast teil an allen äußeren gaben, aber du
        wie keiner, kein du – programmiert flimmert dein herz.

53 Shakespeare x Draesner x Cheesman

what is your substance, what's the stuff you're made of,
that millions of demented chatshows browse on you?
for every single host has one, singly each host one, one's single chatshow,
and you, one single only you, can each and every chatshow over-endue?
portray the fit adonis, and his fabric-stretching silver bromide loins
but laser-print a poorly simulated pseudo-you:
use photoshop™ to brighten up the face of helen, hell,
you once again, on the slide arrayed in your reeking rubber overall.
speak of the year's beginning and its yield,
the former bears the marks of your cell motility,
the latter looks like your manifold gravidity,
and you, in every pregnant shape we make you take,
partake in all apparent giftedness, but only in the part,
ah but you, of no one, no you – just a bug-free, blueprint heart.

55

NOt marble, nor the guilded monument,
Of Princes shall out-liue this powrefull rime;
But you shall shine more bright in these contents
Then vnswept stone, besmeer'd with sluttish time.
When wastefull warre shall *Statues* ouer-turne,
And broiles roote out the worke of masonry,
Nor *Mars* his sword, nor warres quick fire shall burne:
The liuing record of your memory.
Gainst

SHAKE-SPEARES.

Gainst death, and all obliuious emnity
Shall you pace forth, your praise shall stil finde roome,
Euen in the eyes of all posterity
That weare this world out to the ending doome.
    So til the iudgement that your selfe arise,
    You liue in this, and dwell in louers eics.

55 Shakespeare

Not marble, nor the gilded monuments
Of princes, shall outlive this powerful rhyme;
But you shall shine more bright in these contents
Than unswept stone, besmear'd with sluttish time.
When wasteful war shall statues overturn,
And broils root out the work of masonry,
Nor Mars his sword nor war's quick fire shall burn
The living record of your memory.
'Gainst death and all-oblivious enmity
Shall you pace forth; your praise shall still find room,
Even in the eyes of all posterity
That wear this world out to the ending doom.
    So, till the judgment that yourself arise,
    You live in this, and dwell in lovers' eyes.

55 Shakespeare x Draesner

marmor nicht noch goldne website-monumente
werden das alphabet des dichtgepackten überdauern
heller wirst in seinen containern du leuchten
als von hündischer zeit besabberte screens.
wenn der krieg des mülls die monumente stürzt
terroristen brücken, dämme, menschen sprengen
werden rasende atombrände nicht noch mars' klingonen
die lebendaufnahmen deines andenkens verbrennen.
gegen tod und viruskill, der alles löscht
gehst flott du an, dein lob saust in die server ein
ins globale netz der nachwelt krakt es aus
die die erde austrägt zum finalen show-down.
   hier lebst du, bis du auferstehst im letzten menü
   – haust in den augen liebender, ein revenue.

55 Shakespeare x Draesner x Cheesman

not marble nor golden monuments on the web
will outlast what's compressed's alphabet;
you'll emit brighter light in its containers
than screens blurred by time's dog-breath.
when garbage war fells the monuments,
terrorists blow up bridges, dams, and people,
not martial daleks nor reactor blazes will melt down
the live recordings forming your remembrance.
unfazed by death and all-erasing viruscide you stride,
your praise infesting the servers, krakening forth
across the global network of posterity
that bears and wipes the earth in the grand finale.
you live on here, until, in the shut-down drop-down menu,
you arise, at home in lovers' eyes, their re-venue.

60

Ike as the waues make towards the pibled fhore,
So do our minuites haften to their end,
Each changing place with that which goes before,
In fequent toile all forwards do contend.
Natiuity once in the maine of light.

E   Crawls

SHAKE-SPEARES

Crawles to maturity,wherewith being crown'd,
Crooked eclipfes gainft his glory fight,
And time that gaue,doth now his gift confound.
Time doth tranffixe the florifh fet on youth,
And delues the paralels in beauties brow,
Feedes on the rarities of natures truth,
And nothing ftands but for his fieth to mow.
   And yet to times in hope,my verfe fhall ftand
   Praifing thy worth,difright his cruell hand.

60 Shakespeare

Like as the waves make towards the pebbled shore,
So do our minutes hasten to their end;
Each changing place with that which goes before.
In sequent toil all forwards do contend.
Nativity, once in the main of light,
Crawls to maturity, wherewith being crown'd,
Crooked eclipses 'gainst his glory fight,
And Time, that gave, doth now his gift confound.
Time doth transfix the flourish set on youth,
And delves the parallels in beauty's brow;
Feeds on the rarities of nature's truth,
And nothing stands but for his scythe to mow.
   And yet, to times in hope, my verse shall stand,
   Praising thy worth, despite his cruel hand.

60 Shakespeare x Draesner

wie wellen sich vorkämpfen an ölpockigen strand
so rasen unsre minuten ihrem ende zu
mit der vorgängerin tauscht jede den platz, robben
gengestört, stürzen sie sich die klippen hinab.
dass wir natefakte sind rückt erst jetzt ins rampenlicht
die halbe glückshaube der geburt, die chromosomen
krumm verdeckt – wenig glorios, unser zeugungsroulette
den jugendjubelrausch als helixtausch fixiert
die zeit uns ins gesicht und konsumiert frisch
von der leber weg das wahrheitsspiel natur, „frei"
traben wir im anthropark dahin; selbst heu
weiß dort, was züchtung heißt.
    drum, du natefakt, ab in meinen letterntrakt
    grauer samen? quatsch, ich nehme dich im achteltakt.

60 Shakespeare x Draesner x Cheesman

like waves fighting up a crude-moiled beach,
is how our minutes race towards their ends;
each swapping places with its predecessor, seals,
gene-messed, they lemm themselves from off the cliffs.
that we are natefactual is only now spot-lit,
birth's half-auspicious caul that shrouds
crooked chromosomes – rather base, our beget-roulette.
youth's zesty glee's a trade of helices time fixes
on our cheeks and makes no bones about consuming
truth and dare game nature, "free"ly we
trot around our anthropark where even oats
know what breeding strains means.
so, you natefact, down, into my compositor's tray,
dismal jism? nope: iambic pants off, mater, let's play.

65

SInce braſſe, nor ſtone, nor earth, nor boundleſſe ſea,
But ſad mortallity ore-ſwaies their power,
E 2   How

SHAKE-SPEARES

How with this rage ſhall beautie hold a plea,
Whoſe action is no ſtronger then a flower?
O how ſhall ſummers hunny breath hold out,
Againſt the wrackfull ſiedge of battring dayes,
When rocks impregnable are not ſo ſtoute ,
Nor gates of ſteele ſo ſtrong but time decayes?
O fearefull meditation, where alack,
Shall times beſt Iewell from times cheſt lie hid?
Or what ſtrong hand can hold his ſwift foote back,
Or who his ſpoile or beautie can forbid?
    O none, vnleſſe this miracle haue might,
    That in black inck my loue may ſtill ſhine bright.

65 Shakespeare

Since brass, nor stone, nor earth, nor boundless sea,
But sad mortality o'ersways their power,
How with this rage shall beauty hold a plea,
Whose action is no stronger than a flower?
O, how shall summer's honey breath hold out
Against the wrackful siege of battering days,
When rocks impregnable are not so stout,
Nor gates of steel so strong, but time decays?
O fearful meditation! where, alack!
Shall Time's best jewel from Time's chest lie hid?
Or what strong hand can hold his swift foot back?
Or who his spoil of beauty can forbid?
    O none, unless this miracle have might,
    That in black ink my love may still shine bright.

65 Shakespeare x Draesner

seit strahlendes, sowie stein, wie boden, wie in mandelbrotküsten
maßloses meer, ölige sterblichkeit mit zahllosen tanks überspült
kriecht schönheit gegen diese wut ins glas des vier-buchstaben-worts
wo handlung nicht stärker ist als die wendung von chlorophyll ins
       licht.
doch wie soll der honigatmende schaumbesatz des sommers aushalten
gegen den sieg der das schlachten zurückerfindenden tage?
wenn undurchdringliche häute und tore aus unleserlichen codes
unter dem ansturm der zeit nachgeben, welcher gedanke:
bis das mögliche im realen erscheint. wo könnte das klarste
zeitgezeugte sich in der eigenen zeitlichkeit bergen?
oder welche hand kann diesen huschenden lammfuß je halten?
wer diesen missbrauch hellster mischung verbieten?
    keiner, außer er tritt in die macht jener wirklichkeit ein
    in der, in diesen tintenstrahl-füßen, nur die eigene folie hell
       scheint.

65 Shakespeare x Draesner x Cheesman

since rads, and rock, and soil, as well as fractal-shored
gross ocean, oily mortality by the countless tank engulf,
beauty crawls against this wrath inside the four-letter-word's retort,
where action is no stronger than the lightward ply of chlorophyll.
yet how should summer's nectared bubble-wrap hold out
against the siege of days that pack new battle-kill?
if impermeable skins and gates made of unreadable codes
give way to time's assault, then, what a thought:
till might be faces really is. where could what's most
self-evident, time-bred, within its very temporality hide?
or whose hand hold back this lamb's hustling hoof?
this exploit of brightest mixing, who forbid?
o, none, but he assume might to make seeming be,
so in these ink-jet feet, shine bright a lone folie.

68

THus is his cheeke the map of daies out-worne,
    When beauty liu'd and dy'ed as flowers do now,
Before thefe baftard fignes of faire were borne,
Or durft inhabit on a liuing brow,
Before the goulden treffes of the dead,
The right of fepulchers, were fhorne away,
To liue a fcond life on fecond head,
Ere beauties dead fleece made another gay:
In him thofe holy antique howers are feene,
Without all ornament, it felfe and true,
Making no fummer of an others greene,
Robbing no ould to dreffe his beauty new,
    And him as for a map doth Nature ftore,
    To fhew faulfe Art what beauty was of yore.

68 Shakespeare

Thus is his cheek the map of days outworn,
When beauty liv'd and died as flowers do now,
Before these bastard signs of fair were born,
Or durst inhabit on a living brow;
Before the golden tresses of the dead,
The right of sepulchres, were shorn away,
To live a second life on second head,
Ere beauty's dead fleece made another gay:
In him those holy antique hours are seen,
Without all ornament, itself, and true,
Making no summer of another's green,
Robbing no old to dress his beauty new;
    And him as for a map doth Nature store,
    To show false Art what beauty was of yore.

68 Shakespeare x Draesner

sein gesicht: total verbrauchter tage clip
als schönheit noch verging wie heute nur nostalgo-flip
bevor die mischungsmendel des hellsten die retorten verließen
und es wagten, auf lebendigen sprossen zu wachsen
bevor das grabmalrecht gecancelt wurde, der toten
goldener zopf, für ein zweites leben in einem
zweiten kopf, bevor der toten hübscher schäfchencode
andren diente, zum nachwuchslosen frohen sex:
an ihm zeigt sich die gute alte zeit der sterblichkeit
ganz ohne ornament, ist er er selbst, naturident
macht keinen neuen sommer sich mit fremdem grün
raubt keine alten leer, um frisch sich anzuziehn
    weißkittel stellen als videoclip ihn aus, unserer „mache"-
    kunst zu zeigen, was schönheit hieß im land „es war einmal".

68 Shakespeare x Draesner x Cheesman

his face: a clip from well and truly worn-out way-back-thens,
when beauty used to pass as only retro-fads do now,
before the mendel-mixes of the brightest quit the glass
and dared to grow on striplings all alive;
before the law of graveyards, golden dreadlock of the dead,
was snipped for the sake of second life in second head,
before their pretty-lambkins-code was re-interpreted
for others to enjoy sex progeny-free:
this displays the good old days, mortality's,
all unadorned, he's he himself, synth-natured,
making no new summer for himself of borrowed green,
nor cleaning out old timers to refresh his threads;
white-coats run him through the video to show our "can-do"
brand of art what beauty meant in "once upon a" land.

147

MY loue is as a feauer longing ſtill,
For that which longer nurſeth the diſeaſe,
Feeding on that which doth preſerue the ill,
Th'vncertaine ſicklie appetite to pleaſe:
My reaſon the Phiſition to my loue,
Angry that his preſcriptions are not kept
Hath left me, and I deſperate now approoue,
Deſire is death, which Phiſick did except.
Paſt cure I am, now Reaſon is paſt care,
And frantick madde with euer-more vnreſt,
My thoughts and my diſcourſe as mad mens are,
At randon from the truth vainely expreſt.
    For I haue ſworne thee faire, and thought thee bright,
    Who art as black as hell, as darke as night.

147 Shakespeare

My love is a fever, longing still
For that which longer nurseth the disease;
Feeding on that which doth preserve the ill,
The uncertain sickly appetite to please.
My reason, the physician to my love,
Angry that his prescriptions are not kept,
Hath left me, and I desperate now approve
Desire is death, which physic did except.
Past cure I am, now reason is past care.
And frantic mad with evermore unrest;
My thoughts and my discourse as mad men's are,
At random from the truth vainly express'd;
    For I have sworn thee fair, and thought thee bright,
    Who art as black as hell, as dark as night.

147 Shakespeare x Draesner

der liebesfilm, in dem ich schwimme, ist ein fieber
das begehrt, was den verfall fiebrig fördert
und sich von dem nährt, was das ungesunde füttert
um der flimmernden androiden lust zu gefallen.
mein verstand, ehemals der regisseur dieser takes
hat, ärgerlich, dass das schneiden nicht schneller ging
mich verlassen, und ich, verzweifelt, weiß nun
begehren bedeutet tod, auch wenn die regie den körper davon
      ausnimmt.
bin, als machbares, jenseits der möglichkeit, einen schritt
      zurückzumachen
und frenetisch, verrückt, unruhig, endlos
meine gedanken und mein diskurs wie-der-der-verrückt-
en zufällig hie, da, im film der zerschnittenen wahrheit gedacht:
     denn ich habe geschworen, du seist hell, und glaubte, du leuchtest
     du, ein schwarzes loch, unbeherrschbar, endlos, die spirale der
     macht.

147 Shakespeare x Draesner x Cheesman

the love film i'm afloat in is a fever,
desiring what is feverish for decay,
and feeding on what nourishes ill-health,
to tickle on-screen androids' xeno-lust.
my mind, the ex-director of these shots,
annoyed because the editing took so long,
has left me, and now i despairing know
desire means death, even if the auteur exempts the body from it.
i'm, being doable, past stopping to double even one step back,
and frenetically, madly, restless relentlessly
my thoughts and my discourse as of the re-maddened,
chancing here, there, in the film recalling truth cropped low:
for i swore by your brightness, and believed you did glow,
you, a black hole, illimitable, the master coil of power's laminar flow.

Table of Contents

* * *